TECHNICAL REPORT

Naval Aviation Budgeting

Cost Adjustment Sheets and the
Flying Hour Program

Edward G. Keating, Sarah H. Bana, Michael Boito

Prepared for the United States Navy

RAND NATIONAL DEFENSE RESEARCH INSTITUTE

The research described in this report was prepared for the United States Navy. The research was conducted within the RAND National Defense Research Institute, a federally funded research and development center sponsored by the Office of the Secretary of Defense, the Joint Staff, the Unified Combatant Commands, the Navy, the Marine Corps, the defense agencies, and the defense Intelligence Community under Contract W74V8H-06-C-0002.

Library of Congress Control Number: 2012948606

ISBN: 978-0-8330-7688-5

Published 2012 by the RAND Corporation
1776 Main Street, P.O. Box 2138, Santa Monica, CA 90407-2138
1200 South Hayes Street, Arlington, VA 22202-5050
4570 Fifth Avenue, Suite 600, Pittsburgh, PA 15213-2665
RAND URL: http://www.rand.org/
To order RAND documents or to obtain additional information, contact
Distribution Services: Telephone: (310) 451-7002;
Fax: (310) 451-6915; Email: order@rand.org

Preface

In the summer of 2011, Arthur Barber, Deputy Director, Assessment Division, N81B, Office of the Chief of Naval Operations, asked the RAND Corporation to undertake a study entitled "Optimizing the Flying Hour Program Cost Projection Process." As the project progressed, the client directed the RAND research team to focus on Cost Adjustment Sheets (CASs) and their role in the Navy's Flying Hour Program (FHP) budgeting process. In recent years, most CASs have increased the FHP budget. In addition, CASs have been far more utilized by the F/A-18 program than by program offices for most other types of naval aircraft. RAND assessed the contribution of CASs to the accuracy of FHP budgets and whether CAS usage is correlated with expenditure-per-flying-hour growth. RAND also examined why CASs have been used more heavily by the F/A-18 program.

This research should be of interest to Navy and other Department of Defense personnel involved with aviation budgeting issues. It was sponsored by the United States Navy's Assessment Division, N81, and conducted within the Acquisition and Technology Policy Center of the RAND National Defense Research Institute, a federally funded research and development center sponsored by the Office of the Secretary of Defense, the Joint Staff, the Unified Combatant Commands, the Navy, the Marine Corps, the defense agencies, and the defense Intelligence Community.

For more information on the RAND Acquisition and Technology Policy Center, see http://www.rand.org/nsrd/ndri/centers/atp.html or contact the director (contact information is provided on the web page).

Contents

Figures

Tables

Summary

In this report, we examine Cost Adjustment Sheets (CASs) that modify the Navy's Flying Hour Program (FHP) budget to assess whether process reforms may be appropriate.

CASs modify the FHP "baseline budget" of a Type Model Series (T/M/S). There are two ways in which a T/M/S baseline budget is formulated: For a newer aircraft lacking representative historical data, the T/M/S managers develop a budget more than a year in advance of the budgetary execution year based on expert insight and judgment including experiences with analogous aircraft. For older aircraft, prior annual costs (or expenditures) per flying hour (CPH) serve as the foundation of the baseline budget. After formulation of each T/M/S baseline budget—but before commencement of the year of budgetary execution—program managers, Integrated Weapons System Team leads, and fleet class desk representatives are responsible for researching relevant aircraft support issues and, if necessary, developing CASs that modify what then becomes the execution budget (XB), the last budget formulated before a fiscal year commences.

CAS usage varies considerably across T/M/Ss. The F/A-18 makes much greater proportional use of CASs than other T/M/Ss, relative to its share of the Navy aviation budget or Navy aviation expenditures. Use of CASs may not suggest anything unusual about a T/M/S cost structure or growth as much as it suggests delays in ascertaining a change to the T/M/S CPH. CASs can be submitted to reflect initiatives that are projected to reduce costs; they are also submitted to reflect modifications to in-service aircraft that are expected to incur operating and support costs, as well as transitions from one source of repair (such as interim contractor support) to another source (such as organic repair).

The report has three major sections. First, we discuss CASs and how the Navy aviation community uses them. Second, we note the sometimes considerable differences between Navy aviation budgets (which are affected by CASs) and Navy aviation expenditures. Third, we examine expenditure-per-flying-hour growth across different Navy aircraft. We find that while the F/A-18 program makes much more use of the CAS process than other Navy aircraft, there has been nothing unusual about its expenditure-per-flying-hour growth.

An Analysis of Cost Adjustment Sheets

A given CAS affects the XB once, with a one-year lag between the XB and the CAS program objective memorandum (POM), e.g., a POM-11 CAS changed the CPH distribution in the XB for fiscal year 2010 (FY10). Yet CASs generally display projected cost change information across multiple fiscal years, preceding, including, and subsequent to the budget-affected (or XB) fiscal year.

CAS-projected changes for years subsequent to the budget-affected fiscal year may be handled in different ways. One possibility is that the projected changes will be incorporated into the T/M/S baseline budgets. A second possibility is that an updated CAS will be issued in a subsequent year. A third possibility is that the projected out-year change never occurs. If we do not see a subsequent year CAS on the same subject, we cannot tell if the projected change was absorbed into baseline budgets or was abandoned.

There is a lag between formulation of CASs and formulation of the XB. In most cases, CAS values from the budget-affected year enter the XB without substantial alteration. Those CAS-to-XB alterations that do occur tend to be toward moderation, i.e., budget increases tend to become smaller.

The dollar value of F/A-18-related CAS-driven changes in XB has been disproportionate to that program's share of the FHP budget. Indeed, in both FY08 and FY09, the F/A-18 represented more than 100 percent of XB net dollar adjustments, i.e., other Navy T/M/Ss had net budget-reducing adjustments but were offset in aggregate by budget-increasing F/A-18 adjustments. F/A-18 XB adjustment dollar values have been considerably greater than the F/A-18's share of the naval aviation depot-level reparable (AVDLR) and consumables budget, of naval AVDLR and consumables expenditures, and of naval aviation modification (APN-5) appropriations.

While CASs change Navy XBs, the actual amount spent often differs from what is in those budgets, as we discuss next.

Differences Between Budgets and Expenditures

Because of overseas contingency operations, the F/A-18 fleet has repeatedly flown more hours than it has been budgeted to fly. Also, based on receipt of contingency operations supplemental funding, in FY06–10, it had greater AVDLR and consumables expenditures than for which it was budgeted. That pattern changed in FY11, with the F/A-18 spending less than its AVDLR and consumables budget despite overexecuting its FHP.

F/A-18 AVDLR and consumables expenditures per flying hour have consistently come in under budget, with that difference growing in FY11. F/A-18 CASs have increased the six F/A-18 variants' XBs. Therefore, for FY06–10, the gap between AVDLR and consumables budgets and expenditures would have been greater had the CASs not been utilized. In FY11, the F/A-18 AVDLR and consumables budget with CASs exceeded expenditures; without CASs, it would have fallen below expenditures.

Next we examine the extent to which F/A-18 expenditure-per-flying-hour growth has been unusual relative to other aircraft.

Expenditure-per-Flying-Hour Growth by T/M/S

We examined expenditure-per-flying-hour growth across a number of aircraft and found that observed rates of growth of F/A-18 CPH are not unusual compared to other Navy and

Air Force aircraft. So while the F/A-18 program has used CASs more intensively than other T/M/Ss, F/A-18 CPH has not grown unusually.

The MH-53E has had considerable CPH growth, but has only used CASs modestly. So usage of the CAS process is neither a necessary nor a sufficient condition for high growth in CPH.

Conclusions

We are left with two possibilities as to why the F/A-18 program has made so much greater proportional use of the CAS process than almost any other naval aviation T/M/S. One possibility is that there is something intrinsic to the F/A-18—perhaps its acquisition strategy, mission, or point in the lifecycle—which makes it prone to CAS usage. Another possibility is that the F/A-18 program office has evolved to a norm of using CASs for budgetary changes that other T/M/S managers either build into baseline budgets or ignore altogether.

Ultimately, CAS usage (or lack thereof) is not of pre-eminent importance in identifying problematic T/M/Ss. Using the metric of CPH growth, the F/A-18 does not stand out either favorably or unfavorably.

Acknowledgments

The authors appreciate the research sponsorship of Arthur Barber, Deputy Director, Assessment Division, N81B, Office of the Chief of Naval Operations.

Lieutenant Commander Murat "Rick" Sarisen was a very involved and enthusiastic point of contact. We are most appreciative of his extra efforts on our behalf. We received extensive assistance from Marlin "Brad" Buehler of the Patuxent River Naval Air Station Cost Department on this research. Mr. Buehler is extraordinarily well informed about the CAS process and was generous in sharing his time and knowledge with us. We are very grateful for his assistance. Buehler's Patuxent River colleagues Del Burnett, Tim Conley, R.L. Gage, Doug Monin, and Jason Mushrush also assisted us. We also appreciate the assistance of Captain Scott E. Dugan, Captain James J. Fisher, Commander James A. Corlett, Commander Chris J. Demchak, Commander Harold W. DuBois, Commander Douglas R. McLaren, Commander Peter L. Morrison, Commander Doug D. Pfeifle, Commander Angel G. Salinas, Lieutenant Commander Scott Russell, Carlton R. Hill, Dennis Roy, and Stephen Williams. We also received assistance from Brent Boning and Jim Jondrow of the Center for Naval Analyses.

Professor Diana I. Angelis of the Naval Postgraduate School and our RAND colleague John Schank provided thoughtful and constructive reviews of an earlier version of this paper.

Program director Cynthia R. Cook and deputy program director Paul DeLuca provided valuable feedback to the project team as did our colleague Irv Blickstein. Susan Paddock provided statistical advice. Alvie Vickers and Hosay Yaqub provided administrative assistance. Benson Wong helped prepare this document; Arwen Bicknell edited it.

Abbreviations

AVDLR	Aviation Depot-Level Reparable
BES	Budget Estimate Submission
CAS	Cost Adjustment Sheet
CNAF	Commander, Naval Air Forces
CPH	Cost Per Flying Hour
DoD	Department of Defense
ECP	Engineering Change Proposal
FHP	Flying Hour Program
FY	Fiscal Year
LECP	Logistics Engineering Change Proposal
MSD	Material Support Date
NAVAIR	Naval Air Systems Command
PB	President's Budget
POM	Program Objective Memorandum
SE	Standard Error
T/M/S	Type Model Series
XB	Execution Budget

CHAPTER ONE

Introduction

The Navy, like other military services, has a multiyear budgeting process. As that budgeting process advances toward creation of a final or execution budget (XB), there are various opportunities for the information and assumptions undergirding the budget to be updated. One of those opportunities lies in "Cost Adjustment Sheets" (CASs),[1] the focus of this report.

The Office of the Chief of Naval Operations develops a Flying Hour Program (FHP) "baseline budget" for each Type Model Series (T/M/S) more than 12 months in advance of the budgetary execution year, based on the prior year's expenditure data and flying-hour inputs from the Commander, Naval Air Forces (CNAF). A baseline budget assumes a baseline level of flying hours provided by CNAF, e.g., without inclusion of flying hours associated with unexpected military contingencies. A baseline budget for fiscal year (FY) 2012 was likely formulated during the summer of 2010 as part of the budget estimate submission (BES) process. The BES feeds the president's budget (PB), in which the president proposes spending levels for the fiscal year commencing later that same calendar year (e.g., PB 2012 was proposed in February 2011 for FY12 commencing October 1, 2011).

CASs modify a T/M/S baseline budget. There are two ways in which a T/M/S baseline budget is formulated:

- For a newer aircraft lacking representative historical data, the T/M/S managers develop a budget in advance of the budgetary execution year based on expert insight and judgment including experiences with analogous aircraft.
- For older aircraft, prior year actual cost (or expenditures) per flying hour (CPH) serves as the basis of the baseline budget.

After formulation of each T/M/S baseline budget (but before commencement of the year of budgetary execution), program managers, Integrated Weapons System Team leads, and fleet class desk representatives are responsible for researching relevant aircraft support issues and, if necessary, developing CASs that modify what then becomes the XB, i.e., the last budget formulated before a fiscal year commences. For example, CASs for program objective memorandum (POM) year 2013 were approved in December 2010, which led to changes in what became the FY12 XB. There is a one-year offset, e.g., a POM-13 CAS affects the FY12 XB. The XB is the last budget formulated before a fiscal year commences and is the budget against which expenditures occur. Table 1.1 summarizes this calendar.

---

[1] The nomenclature "cost" adjustment sheet is something of a misnomer. CASs adjust budgets, reflecting changes in information about how much the Navy will end up spending. CASs do not literally adjust costs; they reflect changes in projected expenditures.

Table 1.1
The Flying-Hour Budget Development Calendar

FY	Baseline Budget Set	CASs	President's Budget (PB)	Execution Budget (XB)	Fiscal Year Commences	Fiscal Year Concludes
FY09	Summer 2007	December 2007: POM-10 CASs approved	Early calendar 2008	Finalized Summer 2008	October 1, 2009	September 30, 2009
FY10	Summer 2008	December 2008: POM-11 CASs approved	Early calendar 2009	Finalized Summer 2009	October 1, 2009	September 30, 2010
FY11	Summer 2009	December 2009: POM-12 CASs approved	Early calendar 2010	Finalized Summer 2010	October 1, 2010	September 30, 2011
FY12	Summer 2010	December 2010: POM-13 CASs approved	Early calendar 2011	Finalized Summer 2011	October 1, 2011	September 30, 2012
FY13	Summer 2011	December 2011: POM-14 CASs approved	Early calendar 2012	Finalized Summer 2012	October 1, 2012	September 30, 2013
FY14	Summer 2012	December 2012: POM-15 CASs approved	Early calendar 2013	Finalized Summer 2013	October 1, 2013	September 30, 2014

Table 1.1 suggests one reason for CASs: Sometimes required adjustments become known too late for inclusion in the baseline budgets, but prior to commencement of the applicable fiscal year. A program office's use of CASs may not suggest anything unusual about a T/M/S cost structure or growth as much as it suggests delays in ascertaining a T/M/S budgetary situation. A given T/M/S could have considerable year-to-year budgetary growth without any CASs if that growth were reflected in its baseline budgets.

U.S. Naval Air Systems Command (NAVAIR) 4.2 categorizes CASs into five major categories: baseline budget, contract support, fleet-awarded contract, Logistics Engineering Change Proposal (LECP), and general cost adjustment.[2] A baseline budget CAS is submitted for new aircraft without a representative historical CPH. A contract support CAS is submitted for T/M/Ss with minimal or no organic support. This type of CAS is reevaluated and resubmitted every year based on the terms of the contract. While baseline budget and contract CASs are a significant portion of the CAS budget, we do not focus on them in this report because they are fundamentally different, i.e., they start from baselines of zero as opposed to modifying and updating a positive budgetary level. (We do, however, include contract-related expenditures in Chapter Four's analysis of expenditure-per-flying-hour growth.)

The other three categories of cost adjustment, on which we will focus in this report, are LECPs, fleet-awarded contracts, and general cost adjustments. LECP CASs are almost always budget decreases. Fleet-awarded contracts are for maintenance technicians. The general cost adjustment category comprises most types of CASs: systems reaching Material Support Date (MSD); Engineering Change Proposals (ECPs); maintenance concept changes to different levels of maintenance; reliability degradation; reliability improvements; warranty expiration or initiation; or any event or change that temporarily affects aviation depot-level reparable (AVDLR), maintenance, and/or consumables costs significantly. General cost adjustment CASs can reflect either budget increases or budget decreases and would not be reflected in a prior year's XB. Only support changes that significantly affect the future CPH as compared to the base year CPH need to be submitted on a CAS. The Navy provided RAND with a

---

[2]   This paragraph and the next draw information from Buehler (2011).

database of historical CASs, which we draw upon repeatedly in the analysis presented in this report.

CASs can be quite granular, e.g., they can focus on a change affecting one specific part on one or more T/M/Ss. Table 2.1 in the next chapter, for instance, presents a POM-11 CAS concerning flight control surfaces on F/A-18As, F/A-18Bs, F/A-18Cs, and F/A-18Ds. As a result, one can see multiple CASs affecting a single T/M/S in a fiscal year.

CAS usage is not undesirable per se. As shown in Chapter Three, CASs appear to increase the accuracy of T/M/S budgets relative to a case of not having CASs and the new information they provide. But they elicit concern, if only because they more often reflect cost increases. CASs do not, however, cause cost increases.

The remainder of this report is structured as follows: In Chapter Two, we provide an analysis of CASs. Chapter Three discusses differences between budgets and expenditures. Chapter Four discusses CPH growth by T/M/S. Chapter Five presents conclusions.

An Analysis of Cost Adjustment Sheets

This chapter presents examples of CASs and notes how they are used to modify Navy aviation budgets. We also note the historical evolution of CASs, i.e., they tend to call for budget increases rather than decreases. We then examine how the F/A-18 program has made much greater use of CASs than observed in other Navy aircraft programs.

As noted in Table 1.1, a given CAS affects the XB once, with a one-year XB lag behind the CAS POM cycle. For example, a POM-11 CAS altered the FY10 XB, a POM-12 CAS affected the FY11 XB, and so forth. Yet, as illustrated in Table 2.1, CASs generally display information across multiple fiscal years—preceding, including, and subsequent to the budget-affected fiscal year.[1]

Table 2.1's illustrative CAS has both AVDLR and maintenance/consumables[2] cost increases in every fiscal year between FY09 and FY15, i.e., "to be" levels are greater than "as is" levels.[3] However, the FY09 change is not actionable because FY09 was already ongoing in late calendar year 2008 when this CAS was created. Such information may, however, help explain

Table 2.1
An Example: POM-11 F/A-18A-D Flight Control Surfaces CAS (in thousands of 2008 dollars)

FY	AVDLR As Is	AVDLR To Be	Delta AVDLRs	Delta in XB	Consumables As Is	Consumables To Be	Delta Consumables	Delta in XB
FY09	14,089	22,004	+7,914		1,143	1,785	+642	
FY10	**15,363**	**73,192**	**+57,829**	**+52,674**	**1,247**	**1,759**	**+513**	**+466**
FY11	15,013	60,045	+45,052		1,218	2,011	+793	
FY12	15,016	77,973	+62,958		1,218	1,974	+755	
FY13	14.474	55,613	+41,138		1,175	1,898	+724	
FY14	11,440	33,850	+22,410		928	1,546	+618	
FY15	10,179	35,353	+25,174		826	1,527	+701	

---

[1] POM-11 information is used to generate the FY11 total obligation authority level. Hence, in Navy comptroller vernacular, FY11 was the "primary year" from the POM-11 cycle. However, we coin the term "budget-affected" to note that a POM-11 CAS like the one in Table 2.1 changes the FY10 XB.

[2] Consumables do not include fuel costs.

[3] In CAS vernacular, the "as is" level refers to the budgetary baseline the CAS is adjusting. The "to be" level is the budget level to which the CAS recommends changing. However, as we note in Table 2.3, "to be" levels in "out years," i.e., non-budget-affected years, rarely become "as is" levels for a future CAS on the same subject.

a deviation between budget and expenditure levels in FY09. (See Chapter Three for an analysis of budgets versus expenditures.)

We have boldfaced the FY10 row in Table 2.1 because this is the budget-affected year for a POM-11 CAS. Interestingly (and in accord with the more common direction of change—see Table 2.5), the AVDLR and consumables deltas that ended up going into the FY10 XB were somewhat less than indicated in the CAS. We have only included values in the "Delta in XB" columns for FY10 because FY10 is the only year a POM-11 CAS changed the XB.

CAS-projected changes for years subsequent to the budget-affected fiscal year may be handled in different ways. One possibility is that the projected changes will be incorporated into the T/M/S baseline budgets (e.g., the FY11 baseline budget had yet to be finalized when POM-11 CASs were produced). A second possibility is that an updated CAS will be issued in a subsequent year, e.g., a POM-12 CAS on this subject will have FY11 as its budget-affected fiscal year.[4] One frequently sees the same CAS across multiple POM cycles. Table 2.2 provides an example of this.[5]

CASs across POM cycles are not internally consistent, i.e., the "to be" levels in a POM cycle N CAS do not necessarily (or generally) become the "as is" levels in a POM cycle N+1 CAS. Table 2.3, again using LECP 78, illustrates this.

POM-09 showed this CAS with a sizable investment in fiscal year 2007 followed by sizable budgetary savings in FY08–13. But then this CAS reappeared in POM-10, with the sizable investment shifted to 2008 and savings appearing FY09–15. Note that the POM-09 "to be" values for FY08–13 did not transfer to become "as is" values in the POM-10 version of this CAS. Indeed, the POM-10 "as is" values for FY08–13 were quite a bit greater than the POM-09 "as is" (to say nothing of the POM-09 "to be") values.

We are not aware of any guidance or requirement for whether a future year change should be simply absorbed into the baseline budget as opposed to being presented in a subsequent year's CAS. Both approaches appear to be used.

A third possibility is that the projected out-year change simply never occurs, e.g., when a POM-11 CAS was formulated, a given FY12 budget change was anticipated, but was never

Table 2.2
Logistics Engineering Change Proposal 78 H-60 Altitude Heading Reference System Gyro: A CAS Observed over Multiple Cycles

POM Cycle	Budget-Affected Year	AVDLR As Is (in thousands)	AVDLR To Be (in thousands)	AVDLR Delta (in thousands)	Delta in XB (in thousands)
2009	FY08	5,119	346	-4,773	-5,947
2010	FY09	12,664	295	-12,369	-12,216
2011	FY10	6,251	2,309	-3,942	-3,365
2012	FY11	469	162	-307	-224

4   Indeed, as shown in the bottom row of Table 2.5, there was a POM-12 F/A-18A-D Flight Control Surfaces CAS.

5   In Table 2.2's case, we are virtually certain we are seeing the same CAS across different POM cycles due to the distinctive "Logistics Engineering Change Proposal 78" labeling. Other cases, however, are less clear, with subtle changes in CAS titles that may or may not suggest changes to what is being analyzed. When two members of the project team tried to independently create lists of "matched CASs," we had widespread discrepancies, though we matched on Table 2.2's example. We recommend that CASs be assigned specific alphanumeric codes to abet efforts to identify CASs that reoccur.

Table 2.3
Logistics Engineering Change Proposal 78 H-60 Altitude Heading Reference System Gyro: Different POM Cycles' Values for Different Fiscal Years

FY	POM-09 AVDLR As Is (in thousands)	POM-09 AVDLR To Be (in thousands)	POM-10 AVDLR As Is (in thousands)	POM-10 AVDLR To Be (in thousands)
2007	5,371	25,617		
2008	5,119	346	14,102	15,233
2009	4,718	363	12,664	295
2010	4,252	321	11,705	250
2011	3,270	268	10,265	239
2012	2,260	121	8,376	173
2013	1,328	49	5,513	94
2014			2,884	44
2015			1,171	8

implemented, based on subsequent policy changes. If we do not see a subsequent year CAS on the same subject, we cannot tell if the projected change was absorbed into baseline budgets or abandoned.

Focusing on budget-affected years, CAS and XB deltas can be either budget increases or budget decreases. However, as shown in Figure 2.1, XB increases have become increasingly common in recent fiscal years.

Figure 2.1
The Number of XB AVDLR and Consumables Cost Adjustments, FY06–12

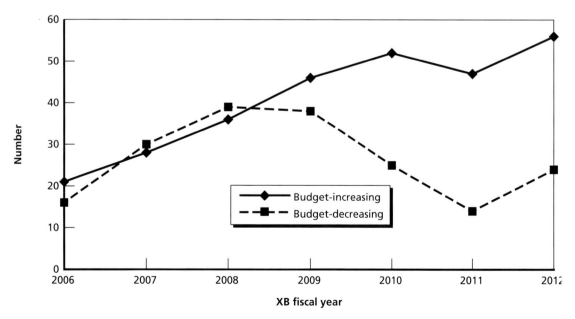

Further, as shown in Figure 2.2, budget-increasing adjustments in XB since FY08 have been of greater dollar value on average than budget-decreasing adjustments.

Figures 2.1 and 2.2 explain the chagrin caused by the CAS process: While Naval Air Enterprise submits CASs showing anticipated cost reductions as well as those with anticipated cost growth, budget-increasing CASs have become increasingly predominant, and those cost adjustments that increase the XB typically have a larger dollar value than those cost adjustments that decrease the XB.

As shown in Figure 2.3, the total dollar value of XB AVDLR and consumables cost adjustments added up to budget increases of around $200 million in FY11 and FY12 after net budget reductions in early years of the CAS process.

We believe that one cannot meaningfully sum "as is" or "to be" values across fiscal years in a single CAS. Likewise, one cannot meaningfully look at a single fiscal year and sum its value across different POM cycles in which that fiscal year is displayed. Table 2.4 illustrates this: Values for FY10 were displayed in CASs all the way between POM Cycle 2005 (when FY10 was a distant out-year) to POM Cycle 2012 (when FY10 had already commenced). Looking solely at F/A-18 AVDLRs and consumables, the CASs repeatedly suggested budget increases. As explained earlier, only one of these adjustments affected a budget (the FY10 XB in the POM-11 CAS cycle).

The POM-11 CASs were the only ones that definitely affected the FY10 F/A-18 XB. Only in POM-11 was FY10 the budget-affected year. It is not clear to us what value is provided by CASs for changes outside the budget-affected year.[6]

Figure 2.2
Average Value of XB Budget-Increasing and Budget-Decreasing AVDLR and Consumables Cost Adjustments, FY06–12

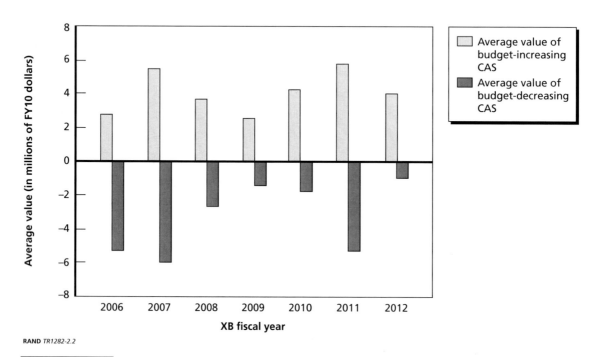

RAND TR1282-2.2

---

[6] One of our reviewers suggested that the out-year changes alert planners and programmers of anticipated changes based on current conditions and assumptions. However, these changes often do not appear in subsequent years' CASs, leading us to question their value.

Figure 2.3
Total Value of XB Budget-Increasing and Budget-Decreasing AVDLR and Consumables Cost Adjustments, FY06–12

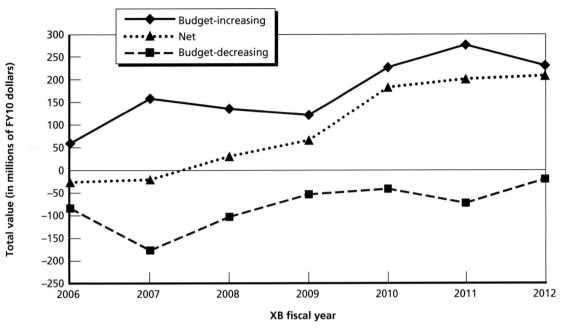

As noted in Table 1.1, there is a lag between formulation of CASs and formulation of the XB. In most cases, as shown in Figure 2.4, CAS values from the budget-affected year enter the XB without substantial alteration. Figure 2.4 covers 438 CASs between 2006 and 2012

Table 2.4
An F/A-18 Illustration of Why One Cannot Cumulate Different Cycles' CASs

POM Cycle	FY10 AVDLR Delta (in thousands)	FY10 Consumables Delta (in thousands)	FY10 AVDLR Delta in XB (in thousands)	FY10 Consumables Delta in XB (in thousands)
2005	+199,751	+2,191		
2006	+297,722	+109,351		
2007	+54,432	+13,574		
2008	+102,218	+5,058		
2009	+88,527	+13,332		
2010	+50,840	+5,902		
2011	+168,779	+13,763	+150,604	+12,326
2012	+116,540	+16,357		
Then-Year Sum	+1,078,808	+179,528		
Total F/A-18 Budget in FY10	**765,512**	**317,601**		
Total F/A-18 Expenditures in FY10	**809,658**	**393,421**		

Figure 2.4
The Observed Relationships Between AVDLR and Consumables CASs and XB Adjustments, 2006–12

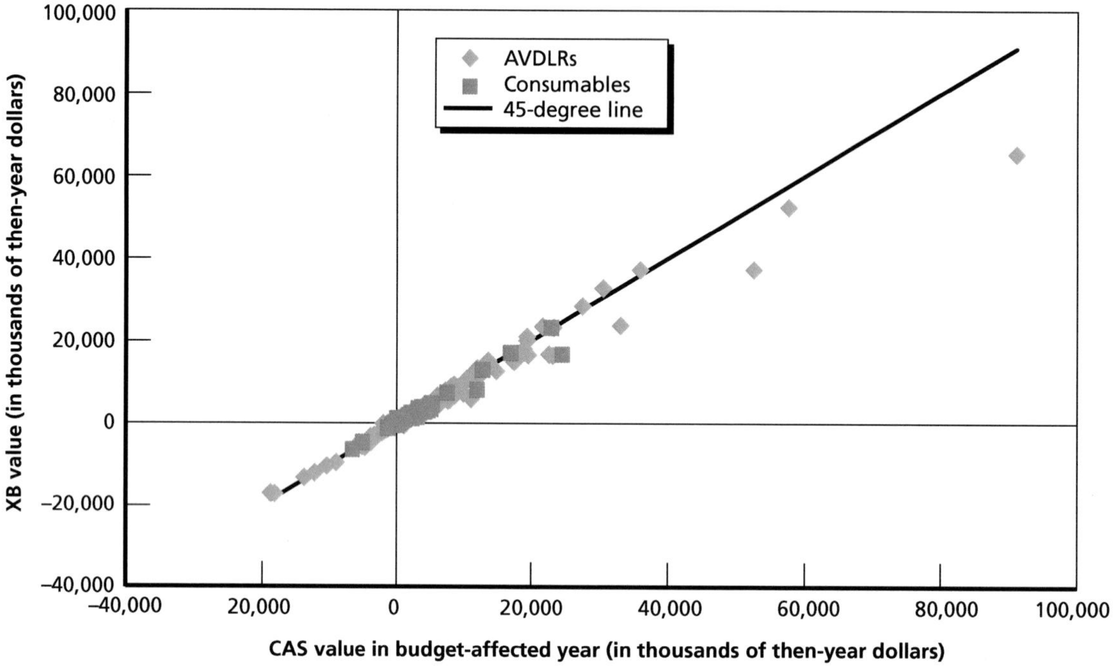

CAS value in budget-affected year (in thousands of then-year dollars)

where we were able to match the CAS's AVDLR and/or consumable value to a corresponding XB adjustment.

In Figure 2.4, an adjustment whose XB value exactly equaled its CAS value would fall on the 45-degree line. Most CASs fall close to the 45-degree line. We expect minor deviations from that line to be caused by, for instance, XB using dollars in different year terms than presented on the CAS forms. There are, however, some icons sufficiently far from the 45-degree line as to not be explained solely by minor differences in inflation adjustments.

A few high-dollar value exceptions are enumerated in Table 2.5. The CAS-to-XB alterations generally appear to be toward budgetary moderation, i.e., XB increases tend to be smaller (closer to zero) so the icon lies under the 45-degree line in Figure 2.4. We also see this pattern toward budgetary moderation in Tables 2.1 and 2.4 and in three of the four rows of Table 2.2.

It is not a coincidence that F/A-18s are prominent in Table 2.5. The six F/A-18 variants are, in aggregate, the Navy's highest annual dollar-value aviation system. Even beyond their level of total spending, the value of F/A-18-related CAS-driven changes in XBs has been disproportionate relative to the F/A-18's share of Navy aviation spending. Figure 2.5 plots the F/A-18's annual share of the AVDLR and consumables XB, the F/A-18's annual share of AVDLR and consumables expenditures, the F/A-18's share of modification appropriations, and, the highest line in Figure 2.5, the F/A-18's net share of XB AVDLR and consumables budget adjustments.[7]

---

[7] Expenditures are what was actually spent as contrasted with the last budget formulated (the XB), against which expenditures occur. We display APN-5 aircraft modification appropriations in Figure 2.5. Not all F/A-18 modifications affecting CAS CPH adjustments have been funded with APN-5 since for F/A-18 aircraft not already delivered, the cost of the modifications was rolled into the APN-1 procurement cost of the aircraft. We use the values of budget adjustments that appear in the XBs, not the sometimes-larger budget adjustments found in CASs.

Table 2.5
High-Dollar-Value Examples Where XB Values Differed from CAS Values

POM Cycle	Budget-Affected Year	CAS	CAS Delta (in thousands)	XB Delta (in thousands)	Cost Category
2011	FY10	F/A-18A-D Flight Control Surfaces	+57,829	+52,674	AVDLRs
2011	FY10	F/A-18E/F IDECM	+19,603	+16,597	AVDLRs
2012	FY11	F/A-18A/C ATFLIR	+22,677	+16,757	AVDLRs
2012	FY11	F/A-18E/F ATFLIR	+33,170	+23,840	AVDLRs
2012	FY11	F/A-18A-D F404 ERF	+23,231	+16,491	AVDLRs
2012	FY11	F/A-18A-D F404 ERF	+12,046	+8,092	Consumables
2012	FY11	EA-18G FIRST Contract Option Renewal	+11,146	+5,760	AVDLRs
2012	FY11	F/A-18A-D Flight Control Surfaces	+52,711	+37,418	AVDLRs

In both FY08 and FY09, the F/A-18's share was more than 100 percent—i.e., other Navy T/M/Ss on net had budget-reducing adjustments but were offset in aggregate by budget-increasing F/A-18 adjustments.[8]

Hence, while the F/A-18 represents roughly one-third of XB and Navy aviation AVDLR and consumables expenditures, and a somewhat lower share of Navy aircraft modification

Figure 2.5
Evidence of Disproportionate F/A-18 Usage of the CAS Process

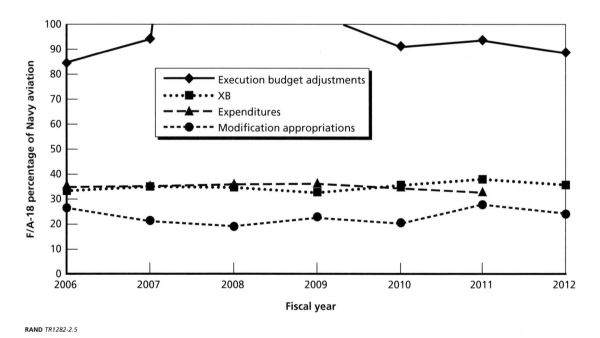

---

[8] We do not extend the vertical axis in Figure 2.5 beyond 100 percent. The 2008 F/A-18 percentage of net XB adjustments exceeded 250 percent, completely obscuring the differences between the XB, expenditure, and modification appropriation percentages illustrated in Figure 2.5.

(APN-5) appropriations, the F/A-18 program has made far more than proportional use of the CAS process to adjust its execution budget.

We did not find any evidence that modifications systematically drive usage of CASs and consequent budget adjustments. Between 1996 and 2011, the F/A-18 received about $6.1 billion (in FY10 dollars) in modification appropriations, or about 19.0 percent of total Navy aviation modification appropriations. The next highest recipients of modification appropriations over that period were the P-3 ($4.8 billion, 14.9 percent) and the EA-6B ($3.3 billion, 10.1 percent). However, as shown in Figure 2.6, the F/A-18 represented 97 percent of net XB AVDLR and consumables budget adjustments over 2006–12, compared with about 1 percent each for the P-3C and the EA-6B.

The P-3C and EA-6B illustrate that modification appropriations do not axiomatically imply high-dollar budget adjustments.

Table 2.6 presents another portrayal of the F/A-18's disproportionate use of the CAS process. The table compares the six F/A-18 variants to the 20 non-F/A-18 T/M/Ss with the greatest FY12 AVDLR and consumables budgets. In FY12, the only other T/M/Ss that remotely used CASs akin to the F/A-18 were the EA-18G and the EA-6B.[9] Several T/M/Ss had no AVDLR or consumables CASs; six of the 20 had net budget-reducing CASs.

Table 2.6 illustrates why our examination of CAS usage in the Navy came to focus on F/A-18 usage of the CAS process.

Figure 2.6
F/A-18, EA-6B, and P-3C Shares of 1996–2011 Modification Appropriations and 2006–12 XB AVDLR and Consumables Net Budget Adjustments

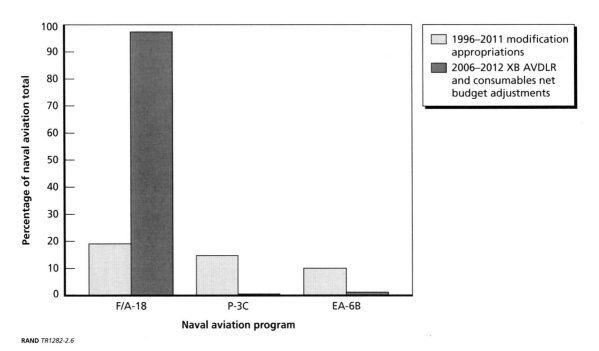

RAND TR1282-2.6

---

[9]   The EA-18G Growler is a variant of the F/A-18F Super Hornet Block II designed to fly airborne electronic attack missions. See Naval Air Systems Command (undated). We learned that EA-18G general cost adjustment CASs are, for all practical purposes, part of the EA-18G baseline budget CAS (but are not labeled as such). For other T/M/Ss, we have removed baseline budget CASs from our analysis.

Table 2.6
FY12 AVDLR and Consumables Budgets and CASs by T/M/S

T/M/S	2012 AVDLR and Consumables Budget (in millions)	2012 XB AVDLR and Consumables Adjustments (in millions)	Adjustment as Percentage of Budget
F/A-18A	113.4	14.9	13.17
F/A-18B	8.1	1.2	14.62
F/A-18C	442.9	60.5	13.66
F/A-18D	206.3	25.7	12.46
F/A-18E	246.4	39.1	15.86
F/A-18F	287.9	44.6	15.48
AH-1W	149.1	-0.7	-0.49
AV-8B	137.0	4.3	3.14
C-130T	28.6	0.0	0.00
C-2A	37.2	-12.2	-32.90
CH-46E	82.4	0.0	0.00
CH-53D	41.8	0.0	0.00
CH-53E	243.3	0.1	0.04
E-2C	81.0	-1.9	-2.30
EA-18G	119.1	26.4	22.13
EA-6B	99.2	8.2	8.31
HH-60H	62.2	-0.1	-0.12
MH-53E	60.8	0.0	0.04
MH-60R	167.6	0.0	0.00
MH-60S	156.6	0.0	0.00
MV-22B	286.1	0.0	0.00
P-3C	174.5	0.7	0.42
SH-60B	155.7	-0.3	-0.18
SH-60F	46.0	-0.1	-0.23
TAV-8B	149.1	0.2	0.11
UH-1N	60.1	0.0	0.00
All Other T/M/Ss	161.4	0.4	0.24

Chapter Summary

While CASs display budget changes across multiple fiscal years, a given CAS only affects the XB once, with a one-year lag to the CAS year (e.g., a POM-11 CAS changes the FY10 XB). CASs across POM cycles are not internally consistent, i.e., the "to be" levels in a POM cycle N CAS do not necessarily (or generally) become the "as is" levels in a POM cycle N+1 CAS.

In recent years, most CASs have reflected budget increases. Further, budget-increasing CASs have tended to have greater dollar value than budget-decreasing CASs.

The F/A-18 program has made disproportionate use of CASs.

Next we discuss the observed differences between XBs (inclusive of CAS-based adjustments) and expenditures.

CHAPTER THREE

Differences Between Budgets and Expenditures

As discussed in Chapter One, the Navy often ends up spending a different amount on maintaining a T/M/S than was budgeted. One possible reason is a change in the number of flying hours due to contingency operations (although there is considerable literature that raises skepticism about the nexus between flying hours and expenditures).[1] Figure 3.1, for instance, compares different T/M/Ss' budgeted versus actual flying hours in FY11. (In this chapter, "budgeted" refers to the final XB.) We have highlighted the six F/A-18 variants using red box icons; other T/M/Ss are displayed as blue diamonds.

Figure 3.1
FY11 Budgeted Versus Actual Flying Hours by T/M/S

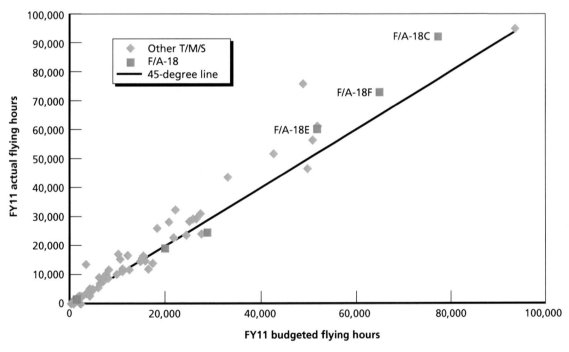

RAND *TR1282-3.1*

---

[1] See, for instance, McGlothlin and Donaldson (1964), Donaldson and Sweetland (1968), Sherbrooke (1997), Wallace, Houser, and Lee (2000), Boning, Goodwyn, and Arriagada (2008), Kirk et al. (2008), and Boning and Geraghty (2009). These studies all suggest that expenditures do not generally change commensurate with changes in flying hours. They also suggest considerable fixed or flying hour-invariant costs in military aviation maintenance.

A T/M/S that flew exactly its budgeted FHP would have its icon lie on the 45-degree line. Descending from right to left, the F/A-18C, F/A-18F, and F/A-18E all flew more hours in FY11 than they were budgeted to fly, i.e., their icons are above the 45-degree line. Along with the three highest flying-hour F/A-18 variants, a number of other Navy T/M/Ss flew more hours than they were budgeted to fly.

Figure 3.2 aggregates the six F/A-18 variants and compares annual budgeted to actual flying hours dating back to 2006. The F/A-18 fleet has repeatedly flown more hours than it was budgeted to fly. The gap was smaller in FY11 than it had been in earlier years.

Despite flying more hours than they were budgeted for the F/A-18E and F variants both underspent their AVDLR and consumables budgets in FY11, i.e., their expenditure levels were less than their budgets. The highest dollar variant, the F/A-18C, had expenditures almost exactly equal to its FY11 AVDLR and consumables budget, the upper right-hand box virtually on the 45-degree line in Figure 3.3.

Figure 3.4 shows that FY11 was the first year in recent history in which F/A-18 AVDLR and consumables expenditures fell below the F/A-18 AVDLR and consumables budget. In FY06–10, the F/A-18 AVDLR and consumables expenditures exceeded the F/A-18 AVDLR and consumables budget. AVDLR and consumables expenditures include contingency and supplemental funding not included in budgets. Budgets include the cost adjustments discussed in Chapter Two. In FY11, the F/A-18 AVDLR and consumables budget increased substantially while F/A-18 AVDLR and consumables expenditures fell modestly in real terms.

Figure 3.2
F/A-18 Budgeted and Actual Flying Hours, FY06–11

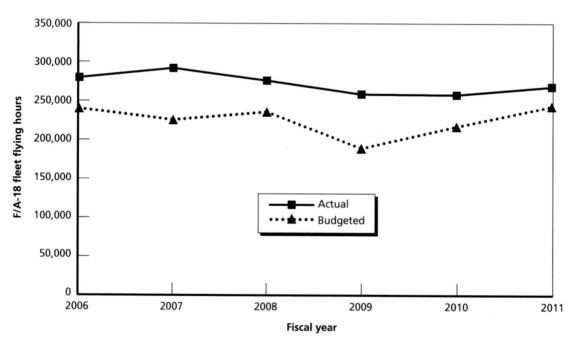

RAND TR1282-3.2

Figure 3.3
FY11 AVDLR and Consumables Budgets Versus Expenditures by T/M/S

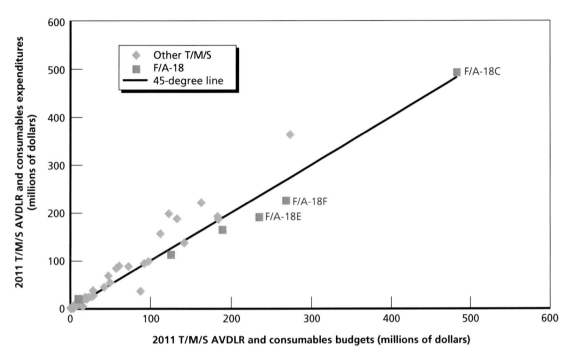

Figure 3.4
F/A-18 AVDLR and Consumables Budgets and Expenditures, FY06–11

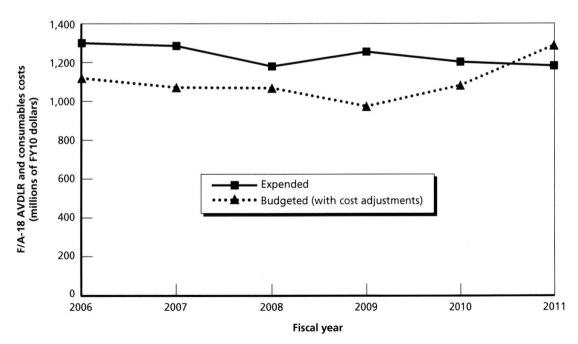

The fact the Navy has been able to repeatedly spend more on F/A-18 AVDLRs and consumables than it had budgeted for has been driven by the availability of contingency funding. The Navy has not violated the Antideficiency Act.[2]

One way to adjust for the increase in F/A-18 flying hours would be to compare AVDLR and consumables budgets per flying hour to expenditures per flying hour by T/M/S. Per-flying-hour adjustments are common in Navy aviation cost analyses. With that normalization, as shown in Figure 3.5, the F/A-18B ($6,437 per flying hour budgeted for AVDLRs and consumables; $12,146 expended per flying hour) is an outlier (due to spending more than $16 million on AVDLRs against a $6 million budget), but the other F/A-18 variants do not stand out. Navy financial experts told us it is not uncommon for a small fleet size T/M/S like the F/A-18B to exceed or underspend its budget sizably in percentage terms.

Figure 3.6 aggregates the six F/A-18 variants, displaying AVDLR and consumables budgets and expenditures per flying hour in constant dollars from 2006–11. Viewed on a per-flying-hour basis, F/A-18 AVDLR and consumables expenditures have run somewhat below budgeted levels, with that gap widening in FY11.

Arguably, however, the flying-hour normalization shown in Figure 3.6 is excessive. Consistent with the literature noted earlier, in the presence of fixed costs, we expect CPH to fall when aircraft fly more. The fact that Figure 3.6's actual per-flying-hour line lies beneath the budgeted per-flying-hour line is in accord with the fixed-cost hypothesis.

Figure 3.5
FY11 AVDLR and Consumables Budgets Versus Expenditures per Flying Hour by T/M/S

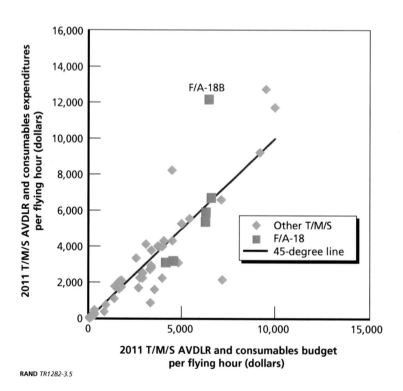

RAND TR1282-3.5

---

[2]   The U.S. Government Accountability Office website (undated) provides background information on the Antideficiency Act.

Figure 3.6
F/A-18 AVDLR and Consumables Budgets and Expenditures per Flying Hour, FY06–11

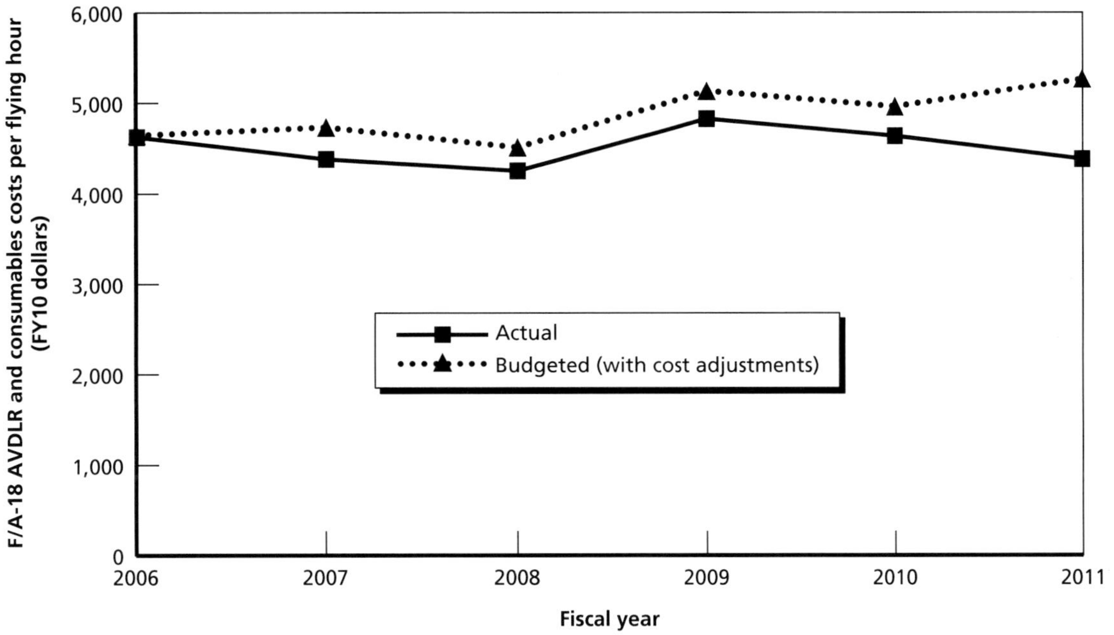

RAND *TR1282-3.6*

F/A-18 CASs have increased the six F/A-18 T/M/Ss' budgets (XBs). Therefore, for FY06–10, the gap between AVDLR and consumables budgets and expenditures would have been greater had the CASs not been utilized.[3] As shown in Figure 3.7, the AVDLR and consumables budget with CASs exceeded expenditures in FY11; without CASs, it would have fallen below expenditures. Expenditures include contingency funding; final or executed budgets (XBs) do not.

As shown in Figure 3.8, AVDLR and consumables budgets per flying hour would have been closer to expenditure levels per flying hour in FY07–09 and in FY11 had the F/A-18 XB not included cost adjustments.

Figure 3.8's peculiar result is driven by a confluence of offsetting factors. Since the F/A-18 has flown more hours than budgeted, there has been downward pressure on its CPH. As noted, flying hours are an imperfect predictor of expenditures and increasing flying hours generally decreases expenditures per flying hours. F/A-18 CASs increased F/A-18 budget levels—so, if those CASs has been ignored, budgeted F/A-18 CPH would have been closer to actual F/A-18 CPH (or expenditures per flying hour).

Of course, we are not in favor of ignoring CASs. They make total budget estimates more accurate than if their information had been ignored. The CAS process provides the opportunity and mechanism for program teams to proactively affect the budgeted CPH of their T/M/Ss by analyzing and estimating CPH impacts of changes in fleet maintenance and

---

[3]   We are not, however, considering the possibility that the CASs themselves allow expenditure levels to be increased. Our assumption, instead, based on discussions with Navy financial experts, is that expenditure levels would have occurred anyway and there simply would have been a greater gap between budgets and expenditure levels absent the CASs.

Figure 3.7
F/A-18 AVDLR and Consumables Budgets and Expenditures, with and without Cost Adjustments, FY06–11

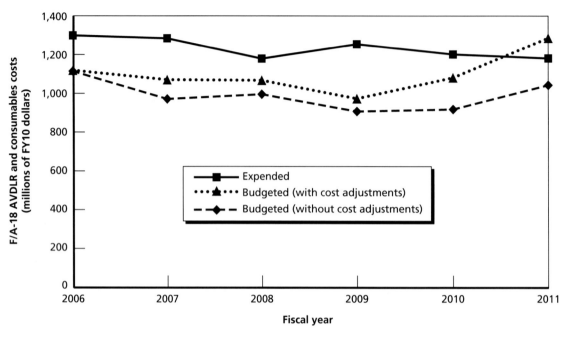

Figure 3.8
F/A-18 AVDLR and Consumables Budgets and Expenditures Per Flying Hour, with and without Cost Adjustments, FY06–11

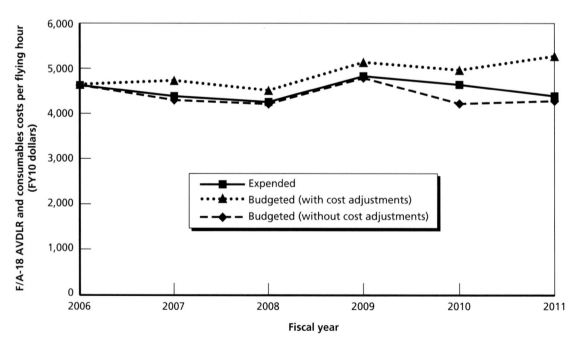

logistics support. Figure 3.8's result would not have occurred without unexpected contingency flying hours.

Chapter Summary

Driven by contingency operations, Navy aircraft, including the F/A-18, have frequently flown more hours than planned for in their budgets. From FY06–10, the F/A-18 also spent more on AVDLRs and consumables than budgeted due to availability of supplemental contingency funding. However, the increase in flying hours has been greater than the increase in spending, so F/A-18 AVDLR and consumables expenditures per flying hour have been lower than budgeted.

If it had not been for CASs, the difference between F/A-18 AVDLR and consumables budgets and expenditures would have been even greater.

Next we analyze expenditures-per-flying-hour growth by T/M/S.

CHAPTER FOUR

Expenditure-per-Flying-Hour Growth by T/M/S

While the F/A-18 program has made greater use of budget-increasing CASs than most other T/M/Ss, there is not necessarily a normative content to this observation. A T/M/S could equally well build increases into its baseline budgets, eschewing CASs altogether or even having budget-decreasing CASs. Or a T/M/S could simply live with inaccurate budgets that chronically underestimate expenditures. The metric of greatest interest in this chapter is how much a T/M/S expends per flying hour, not when and whether those costs are budgeted for. We are especially focused on whether the F/A-18 program, with its high CAS use, stands out with respect to expenditures-per-flying-hour growth.

Figure 4.1 shows F/A-18E/F constant dollar CPH (covering AVDLR, consumables, and, in this chapter, contract expenditures per flying hour) dating back to 1999.[1] CPH in this analy-

Figure 4.1
F/A-18E/F Expenditures per Flying Hour (in FY10 dollars), 1999–2011

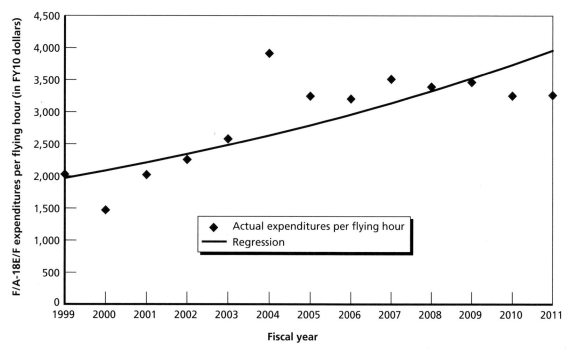

RAND *TR1282-4.1*

---

[1] For this chapter's analysis, we aggregated the A/B, C/D, and E/F variants of the F/A-18. We include contract expenditures in this chapter because they are an important component of some aircraft's total operating costs.

sis does not include fuel costs. Unger (2009) finds the not-surprising result that fuel expenditures, almost uniquely among aviation cost categories, are highly correlated with flying hours, controlling for fuel price levels. Figure 4.1 shows a considerable increase in F/A-18E/F CPH between 2003 and 2004. Since 2004, F/A-18E/F CPH has plateaued in real terms.

Recent years' F/A-18E/F CPH growth may be artificially suppressed by a fixed-price performance-based logistics contract. NAVAIR experts suggested this aircraft's CPH may jump after that contract ends.

Figure 4.1 also shows a curve derived from regression of the natural log of the annual expenditures per flying hour on a constant and the fiscal year. These regression results are shown in Table 4.1.

The Year coefficient of 0.058 is of particular interest. This estimate suggests F/A-18E/F expenditures per flying hour grew at an average annual rate of 5.8 percent between 1999 and 2011.

F/A-18E/F CPH had a particular jump between 2003 ($2,580 per flying hour in FY10 dollars) and 2004 ($3,914 per flying hour). One contributor to this expenditure jump was a 94 percent increase in the F/A-18E/F AVDLR net annual price change in 2004 in the Navy working capital fund pricing system. Figure 4.2 presents NAVAIR-provided data on F/A-18E/F AVDLR price changes in recent years.

Table 4.1
F/A-18E/F CPH Regression Results

Regression Statistics

R Squared	0.6132				
Adjusted R-Squared	0.5780				
Standard Error	0.1883				
Observations	13				

ANOVA	Df	SS	MS	F	Significance F
Regression	1	0.618137	0.618137	17.43778	0.0015
Residual	11	0.389930	0.035448		
Total	12	1.008067			

	Coefficient	SE	T Statistic	P Value
Intercept	-108.914	27.98184	-3.89	0.003
Year	0.058278	0.013956	4.18	0.002

NOTE: Presents standard linear regression outputs. R squared, for instance, is a measure of goodness-of-fit. In this particular case, about 60 percent of the variability in CPH is explained by a time trend, the Year variable. The coefficients are the regression's best fit estimates, e.g., a 5.8 percent estimate of the Year coefficient. The standard error (SE) provides an estimate of the precision of that estimate. The T statistic is the ratio of the coefficient estimate and the SE. The P value for the Year coefficient is very small (sizably below the traditional cutoffs of 0.05 or 0.01), suggesting there is a statistically significant time trend in these data (i.e., the 5.8 percent coefficient estimate is not simply an artifact of randomness in the data).

Figure 4.2
F/A-18E/F AVDLR Annual Price Changes, FY03–12

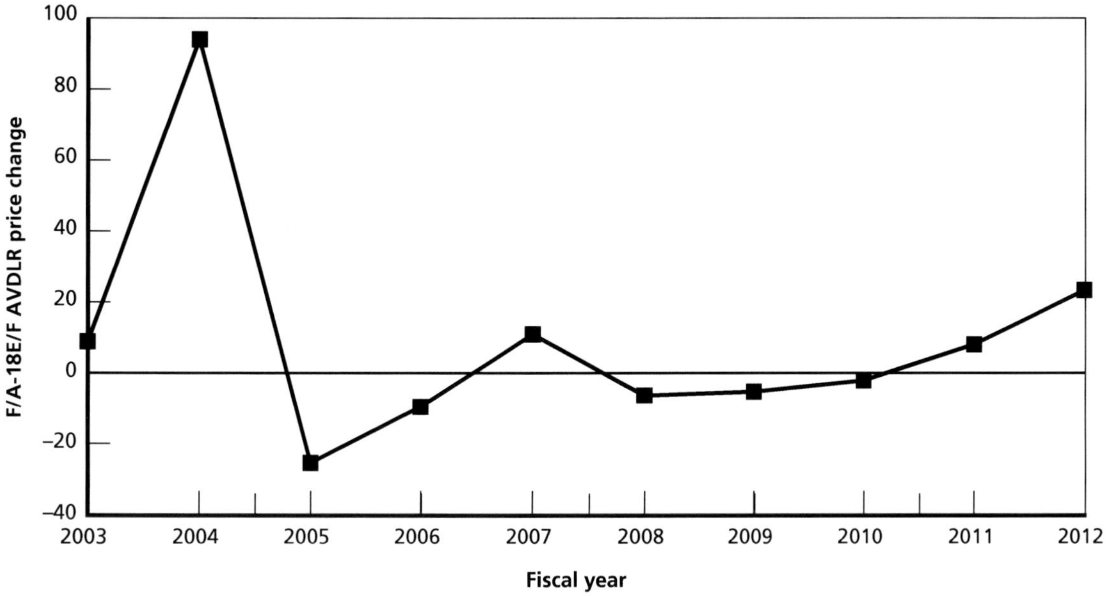

We ran Table 4.1-type regressions for the F/A-18A/B, F/A-18C/D, 30 other Navy T/M/Ss, and five Air Force aircraft.[2] Figure 4.3 presents the 38 regressions' Year coefficients ordered from lowest on the left (–0.1 percent for the EP-3E) to greatest on the right (8.9 percent for the MH-53E). We have highlighted in red the F/A-18A/B (3.1 percent), F/A-18C/D (4.9 percent) and F/A-18E/F (Table 4.1's 5.8 percent).[3] The Air Force aircraft are noted in solid black. Their Year coefficient estimates resemble the Navy aircraft's.

A key insight from Figure 4.3 is that estimated F/A-18 year effects, i.e., their observed rates of growth in CPH, are not unusual compared with other military aircraft. The three F/A-18 pairs have the 11th (F/A-18E/F), 20th (F/A-18C/D), and 28th (F/A-18A/B) largest growth rates out of 38 presented in Figure 4.3.

To more formally test that F/A-18 cost-per-flying-hour growth has not been unusual, we estimated a pooled regression with a common growth rate across all aircraft plus aircraft-specific constant terms. We also included an F/A-18-unique Year variable to test whether F/A-18 CPH growth has been significantly different from other aircraft. As shown in Table 4.2, it has

---

[2]   The 32 Navy non-F/A-18E/F regressions had 18 years of observations (1994–2011) rather than the 13 years of observations (1999–2011) we had for the F/A-18E/F. Inclusion of 1994–98 observations does not appear to have any material effect on coefficeint estimates beyond desirably increasing estimation sample size. The F/A-18C/D Year coefficient estimate, for instance, is 4.9 percent using the 1994–2011 data versus 4.4 percent restricting the data to 1999–2011. The five Air Force regressions cover 1996–2010. The dependent variable in the Air Force regressions was constant-dollar depot-level reparables expenditures per flying hour.

[3]   These year effect estimates are larger than most of the literature's estimates of aircraft aging effects. See, for instance, Dixon (2006). Figure 4.3's year effect estimates include both actual increases in efforts to maintain the aircraft (what we traditionally think of as an aging effect) and financial effects such as Figure 4.2's AVDLR price changes. Aging effect analyses, e.g., Pyles (2003), often focus on hands-on maintenance hours, removing noise caused by changes in maintenance financing approaches. Also, some of Figure 4.3's aircraft had fleet composition changes (aircraft entering and exiting service) during the span of the data, so the year coefficient estimates additionally include fleet composition change effects.

Figure 4.3
Different Navy and Air Force Aircraft Regression-Estimated Year Coefficients

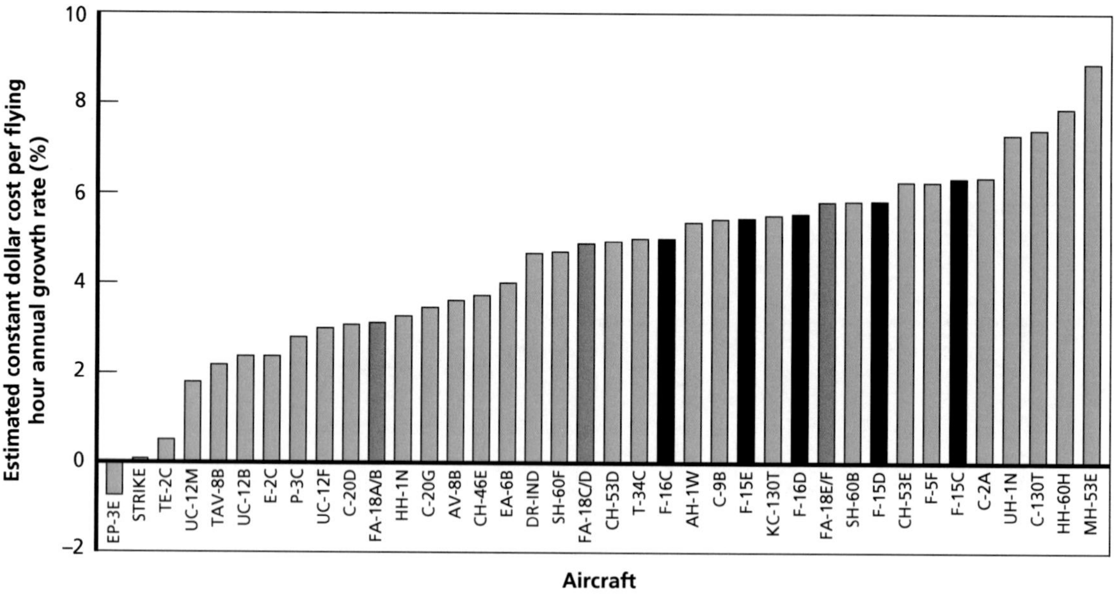

not—i.e., the F/A-18 Year coefficient is highly insignificant. (In the interest of parsimony, Table 4.2 omits the 37 different intercept terms estimated in this regression.)

Table 4.2 suggests an average annual growth rate of about 4.4 percent across the 38 military aircraft, but F/A-18 annual growth has not been significantly different from that pooled mean growth rate.[4]

Drawing together Figure 4.3 and Table 4.2, CPH growth appears to be a nearly ubiquitous occurrence affecting both Navy and Air Force aircraft,[5] independent of whether and to what extent they use the CAS process. While the F/A-18 program has used CASs more intensively than have other T/M/Ss, F/A-18 expenditures per flying hour have not grown unusually. Also recall, for example, from Table 2.6, that all six F/A-18 variants have been heavy users of CASs, but the A/B variants show Year coefficients that are below average in Figure 4.3. CAS submission, all by itself, does not imply large expenditure-per-flying-hour growth.

One explanation for the F/A-18 variants' lack of prominence in Figure 4.3 is the considerable number of flying hours the aircraft has experienced in recent years, noted in Figure 3.2. Based on literature cited earlier, in the presence of fixed costs, we expect CPH to fall as flying hours increase. Of course, contingency operations have increased flying hours, thereby reducing CPH, for many of Figure 4.3's aircraft.

---

[4] The -0.000762 F/A-18 Year coefficient estimate is the best estimate of the difference between the F/A-18 mean growth rate and the pooled mean across all the aircraft. This coefficient is not statistically significantly different from zero, i.e., one cannot reject a null hypothesis that F/A-18 annual growth rates are the same as those of other aircraft.

[5] Jondrow et al. (2003) discussed why depot-level costs per flight hour have increased. Increasing average aircraft ages causing increased numbers of repairs per flight hour is one explanation. Increasingly complex and, hence, costly repair parts is another explanation.

Table 4.2
38 Military Aircraft Pooled CPH Regression Results

Regression Statistics					
R Squared	0.8885				
Adjusted R-Squared	0.8816				
Standard Error	0.2601				
Observations	664				

ANOVA	Df	SS	MS	F	Significance F
Regression	39	336.4984	8.628165	127.55	0.0000
Residual	624	42.2119	0.067647		
Total	663	378.7103			

	Coefficient	SE	T Statistic	P Value	
Intercept	-79.561	4.127506	-19.28	0.000	
[Omit 37 aircraft constant terms]					
Year	0.043714	0.002060	21.22	0.000	
F/A-18 Year	-0.000762	0.007938	-0.10	0.924	

The MH-53E helicopter has the highest constant-dollar CPH growth rate in Figure 4.3. As shown in Figure 4.4, the MH-53E had rising real total expenditures through the 1990s and falling flying hours in the 2000s, combining to create considerable increases in its CPH.

As shown in Figure 4.5, MH-53E CAS usage has been modest.

As illustrated in Table 2.6, the F/A-18 program, by contrast, has repeatedly had AVDLR and consumables cost adjustments whose dollar values have exceeded 10 percent of their annual AVDLR and consumables XB.

The MH-53E and F/A-18A/B examples, respectively, show that extensive use of the CAS process is neither a necessary nor a sufficient condition for high growth in expenditures per flying hour.

Chapter Summary

Compared to other military aircraft, F/A-18 CPH growth has not been unusual. CPH growth appears to be a nearly ubiquitous occurrence, independent of whether and to what extent a T/M/S uses the CAS process. The highest constant-dollar CPH growth rate T/M/S, the MH-53E helicopter, has made only modest use of CASs.

Figure 4.4
MH-53E Actual Flying Hours and Total Expenditures, FY94–11

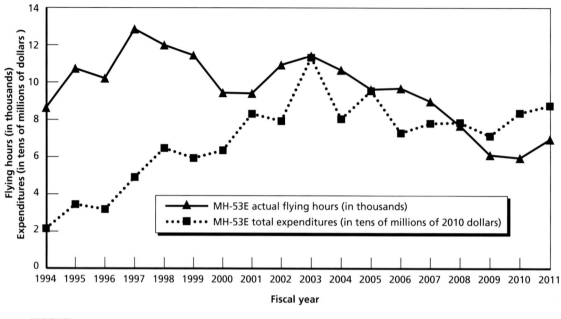

RAND *TR1282-4.4*

Figure 4.5
MH-53E AVDLR and Consumables Cost Adjustments as a Percentage of XB, FY06–12

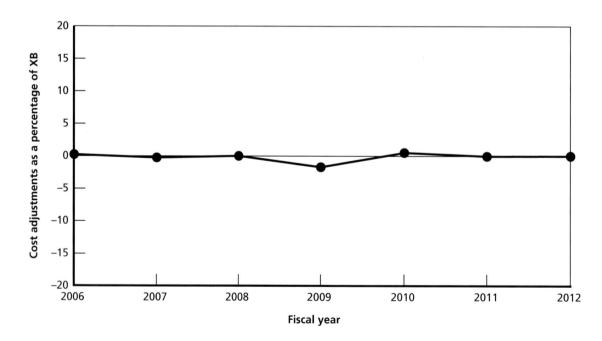

CHAPTER FIVE

Conclusions

In Chapter Two, we showed that the F/A-18 program has made considerable use of the CAS process. In Chapter Three, we showed that these F/A-18 CASs have made their budgets more accurate, at least on a total (rather than on a CPH) basis. In Chapter Four, we showed that F/A-18 CPH growth has not been unusual, i.e., the F/A-18 has not experienced outlier CPH growth despite its unusual usage of the CAS process.

This report has left a major question unanswered: Why has the F/A-18 program made so much greater proportional use of the CAS process than almost any other naval aviation T/M/S? We looked for a relationship between CAS usage and annual spending levels, but the F/A-18's CAS usage is large even compared to its annual spending level. We also explored a hypothesis that modification appropriations drive CASs—but, again, F/A-18 CAS usage is disproportionate relative to its level of modification appropriations.

There appear to be two non-mutually exclusive explanations for F/A-18 CAS usage.

First, there are factors intrinsic to the F/A-18, especially to the E/F, that encourage CAS usage. For instance, the F/A-18E/F has consciously used a spiral development acquisition strategy in which enhancements have been incrementally added to aircraft, many of which then require CAS usage.[1] Also, all F/A-18 variants have been used extensively in recent military conflicts, generating flying-hour and cost adjustments. In addition, the F/A-18E/F has had a number of components hit their MSD, i.e., come off of interim contractor support, thereby generating CASs.

Table 5.1 presents the total number of non-baseline budget and non-contract support CASs for POM05-POM13 by type of aircraft. The table also shows the number and percentage of these CASs attributed to MSD.

The F/A-18 had the largest number of CASs attributed to MSD and the third highest percentage of its non-baseline budget and non-contract support CASs attributed to MSD (behind the EA-18G and the KC-130). Table 5.1 is consistent with a hypothesis that aircraft reaching MSD is one explanation for F/A-18 usage of the CAS process.

Second, we believe that the F/A-18 program has used CASs where other programs have used other approaches. For instance, instead of using topic-specific CASs, budgetary adjustments for newer systems could be built into aggregated baseline budgets. One expert opined that "the V-22 could have 25 CASs per year." (Table 2.6 shows no MV-22B CAS usage in POM-13 affecting FY12.) Another possibility is that other programs have simply allowed their budgets not to be updated with new information by not filing CASs about changes.

---

[1] Younossi et al. (2005) discusses the F/A-18E/F's spiral development acquisition strategy.

Table 5.1
POM05-POM13 Non-Baseline Budget and Non-Contract Support CASs by Aircraft

Aircraft	MSD CASs	Total CASs	MSD Percentage of Total CASs
AH-1W	3	29	10.3
AV-8B	1	67	1.5
C-2A/E-2C	6	138	4.3
CH-46	4	20	20.0
CH-53	5	48	10.4
EA-18G	26	45	57.8
EA-6B	0	26	0.0
F/A-18	72	250	28.8
HH-60	2	24	8.3
KC-130	4	12	33.3
MH-60	0	8	0.0
P-3C	5	68	7.4
SH-60	0	16	0.0
Other Aircraft	11	93	11.8
Total	139	844	16.5 (average)

It may not be important to isolate why F/A-18 CAS usage has been unusual nor, in fact, to change that usage pattern. Ultimately, CAS usage (or lack thereof) is not of pre-eminent importance in identifying problematic T/M/Ss. It is much more important to analyze patterns in T/M/Ss' expenditures. Using the metric of expenditures-per-flying-hour growth, the F/A-18 does not stand out either favorably or unfavorably. It would be worrisome if F/A-18 CPH growth stood out the way its CAS usage does. Fortunately, that is not the case.

References

Boning, William Brent, and Thomas M. Geraghty, *Budgeting for AVDLRs with Fixed Cost*, Alexandria, Va.: CNA Corporation, CRM D0020940.A2/Final, December 2009.

Boning, William Brent, S. Craig Goodwyn, and Leopoldo E. Soto Arriagada, *Causes of the Drop in AVDLR Consumption*, Alexandria, Va.: CNA Corporation, CRM D0016735.A4/1REV, January 2008.

Buehler, Brad, "POM14 Flying Hour Program (FHP) Cost Adjustment Sheet (CAS) Overview," presentation presented to NAVAIR at CAS Submission Information Meeting, Patuxent River, Md., August 22, 2011.

Dixon, Matthew C., *The Maintenance Costs of Aging Aircraft: Insights from Commercial Aviation*, Santa Monica, Calif.: RAND Corporation, MG-486-AF, 2006. As of July 31, 2012:
http://www.rand.org/pubs/monographs/MG486.html

Donaldson, Theodore S., and A.F. Sweetland, *The Relationship of Flight-Line Maintenance Man-Hours to Aircraft Flying Hours*, Santa Monica, Calif.: RAND Corporation, RM-5701-PR, August 1968.

Jondrow, James J., John P. Hall, Rebecca L. Kirk, Geoffrey B. Shaw, Barbara H. Measell, and LCDR Gregory Pederson, *Results on the Cost of the Naval Flight Hour Program*, Alexandria, Va.: Center for Naval Analyses, CAB D0008901.A1/Final, September 2003.

Kirk, Rebecca L., Scott E. Davis, Wm. Brent Boning, Leopoldo Soto Arriagada, Michael D. Bowes, Thomas J. DePalma, Zachary T. Miller, and Jessica S. Oi, *Fixed Cost of Naval Aviation: Exploring Flying Hour Program AVDLR Costs*, Alexandria, Va.: Center for Naval Analyses, CRM D0019011.A2/Final, December 2008.

McGlothlin, William H., and Theodore S. Donaldson, *Trends in Aircraft Maintenance Requirements*, Santa Monica, Calif.: RAND Corporation, RM-4049-PR, June 1964.

Naval Air Systems Command, "Aircraft and Weapons: EA-18G Growler," undated. As of July 31, 2012:
http://www.navair.navy.mil/index.cfm?fuseaction=home.
display&key=33BFA969-0482-42CF-9E1F-F80A1B32BEE9

Pyles, Raymond A., *Aging Aircraft: USAF Workload and Material Consumption Life Cycle Patterns*, Santa Monica, Calif.: RAND Corporation, MR-1641-AF, 2003. As of July 31, 2012:
http://www.rand.org/pubs/monograph_reports/MR1641.html

Sherbrooke, Craig C., *Using Sorties Vs. Flying Hours to Predict Aircraft Spares Demand*, McLean, Va.: Logistics Management Institute, AF501LN1, 1997.

Unger, Eric J., *An Examination of the Relationship Between Usage and Operating-and-Support Costs of U.S. Air Force Aircraft*, Santa Monica, Calif.: RAND Corporation, TR-594-AF, 2009. As of July 31, 2012:
http://www.rand.org/pubs/technical_reports/TR594.html

U.S. Government Accountability Office, "Antideficiency Act Background" website, undated. As of June 2, 2012:
http://www.gao.gov/legal/lawresources/antideficiencybackground.html

Wallace, John M., Scott A. Houser, and David A. Lee, *A Physics-Based Alternative to Cost-Per-Flying-Hour Models of Aircraft Consumption Costs*, McLean, Va.: Logistics Management Institute, AF909T1, August 2000.

Younossi, Obaid, David E. Stem, Mark A. Lorell, and Frances M. Lussier, *Lessons Learned from the F/A-22 and F/A-18E/F Development Programs*, Santa Monica, Calif.: RAND Corporation, MG-276-AF, 2005. As of July 31, 2012:
http://www.rand.org/pubs/monographs/MG276.html